# better gods

www.chuckoneilauthor.com

Copyright © 2024 Chuck O'Neil

# better gods

ISBN: 978-1-957883-14-4 (paperback)
ISBN: 978-1-957883-15-1 (e book)
Library of Congress Control Number:  2024917920


Cover Art: Tatiana Rusakova, Ukraine


StoneBear Publishing LLC - 09/2024
Milford, PA 18337
www.stonebearpublishing.com

**by Chuck O'Neil**

*better gods*

*Holding Things Together*

*Beyond Basilicas*

*Eating Out*

*The Perfect Scar*

# SAWKILL FALLS EDITIONS

*The Falls of the Sawkill*
19th Century
Artist: Signature Illegible

*for Celeste*
*for Ben, Chuck, Beth, Sarah*
*for Lily, Rory, Patrick*

# better gods

Chuck O'Neil

# CONTENTS

## Coda

# better gods

# Whereabouts

Settlements in those days
    were coastal mostly
Built where rivers
    widened into bays

Deep enough
    for the ships
That sailed here
    from other lands

Roads early on
    were the paths they'd found
That ran along shore
    and wound through the woods

They widened them
    rid them of stumps and boulders
And gave them names
    and names to their destinations

And they mapped their whereabouts
    and stood up stones
To say which way
    and how far

And all they gave names to
    they took to be their own
While the pathmakers
    the original ones

Who'd already named
    the many peaks
Inlets   falls   birds
    seasons   flowers   the moon

Snow   the sun   stars
    and names for the snake   fish
Squirrel   fox   bear
    deer   rabbit   bobcat

Who inhabited the valley
    before anybody else
And first to chant at that place
    where the creek becomes the river

About spirit   and fire
    and the ancestors
Were removed   driven out
    by the ones who arrived in ships

And by their seed
    forced west and north
West again   further north
    carrying the ground

And the names
    and the living bones
They'd left behind

# 1

*In silence and stillness the stone*
*Held the memory of the village.*

*Stone is the tabernacle of memory.*

John O'Donohue

# Touchstone

*for Eamon Grennan*


Rescued from the utility crew's heap
When trenching pipe
Through Gooseberry Alley

We stood it in our yard
Beneath the trees
Where the driveway meets the street

And called the cemetery carver
To grave it about belt high
With our house number

Lion-colored among the evergreens
I pull weeds from the mulch
Around its base this morning

In the sway of sun and shade
Place my hand on its cool
Rain-clean skull

Old boulder   up from local clay
Laying groundwork
Reminding me

# Miserere

*for Jim Haggarty*

Here   above town
Walls weave among the trees

Some look like
Rocks tossed together
To get them out of the way

Others   stacked from both sides
One-on-two   two-on-one
Stand as fencing still

And where the hill plateaus
A field long ago

Its view of the valley
Overrun with ramble rose
Clumped with saplings
Shagbark   a few red cedar

Heaven help those
Who are called away

Who leave their labor
When the time comes

Blessed are they who hay the high acres
And keep them clear for years and years

Maker of all days   incline your ear
And according to your mercy

Raise the ones who lift
So many stones

# Rubble

*. . . to take familiar things and make poetry of them*
*in such a way that it looks as if it was easy*
                                Horace   *Ars Poetica*
                                Trans. David Ferry

1
He digs them out
Uses his pry bar
To pick them off the hill
Rolls them with his boot into piles

And when the wheel on the barrow blows
Drags them across the grass on a sled

One fair-sized flat-faced rock
Tucked below spruce limbs
Gives him a look   as if to ask
*What took so long*


2
It's slow going
Working by eye

And from a sketch
He's kept in his head

Misjudging the importance
Of gaps at first
Underestimating   by a lot
How many rocks the wall would take

So he's forever on the hunt
For stones in need of a home
Jobsites   back roads
Fields around his shop
The creeks even


3
He goes out in the morning
And reworks his work
Turning   flipping
Changing one shape for another
Standing back to see

Same stones pretty much
But stacked more like walls
He remembers growing up

And that section he expected
Would give him fits
(The curved place
He's dubbed 'the grotto')
Builds itself almost


4
October sun sinking
A ghost moon low above the trees
The cold growing

He hoses the wall down
From end to end

Loves those wet grays
Tans   mineral streaks

Stones on the loose once   he thinks
What a mason might call rubble
Cobbled the length of the back slope

Holding up
In snows to come

Spilling with vinca
Summers from now

And free of its maker
As though here all along

# Ground Keepers

*remembering Stanley Kunitz*

When your house falls
Into other hands

When sand snows over
The brick-edged terraces

And roses no longer
Swell in sea air

Know we take up the rake
And the spade along with it

And the trowel
And the dented buckets

Weeding by the crushed-shell path
Listening on one knee

Composting   watering   cutting back
Scattering ash as you did

And know we'll hold to it
Bee balm   veronica   anemones

Annuals in clusters
Perennials in their rows

For the length of days
Sowing   staking   making way

Saying our say among the sorrows
Turning the earth as we go

## Watch Hill

1
Another summer ending

Dad and I walk the beach a last time
In the late August back-to-school air

Up the way
A boy yells for his father
To watch him ride a wave
It tumbles him in
Dripping seaweed and sand
And he stands up grinning

The father cheers   laughs and claps
And the boy races back out
To time the next high wave

And Dad says to me as we pass
*You'll never know*
*What it's like to be second*
(He was second of eight
And I his firstborn)

At seventy-one
Thick forearms   vice-grip hands still

An electrician forever
He says   *the only time*
*I felt my dad's love   just for me*
*Was when I was leaving for the war*

*His eyes were wet then*   he says
*And he grabbed me by the arm*
*And warned me*
*To take care of myself over there*

2
Not far from the lighthouse
And Dad says   *you know*
*I never really knew my father*

At a loss   I say   *Dad*
*Maybe you shouldn't take it so personally*
*Because nobody really knew*
*Who Grandpa was*

I'd always heard that
Driving home from Hartford
In a blinding rain
He hit a man
On the side of the road

And was never the same after that
Relied more on his bourbon

'The Old Gent' as he was called
Was the remote wiry Irishman
Who lit a Chesterfield King
After a slice of my mother's apple pie
And   eyeing my captivation
With the rise of his smoke
Shook a finger   and threatened me
*Don't ever smoke*
*It's a damn dirty expensive habit*

3
An air horn chokes
To start an end-of-season race

And looking out to the cluster of sails
Dad recalls words
Written by a commanding officer
He knows by heart

*Sergeant O'Neil can be*
*Trusted implicitly with responsibility*

Out of nowhere   blasting through
Like a relic from World War Two
A prop plane cuts the cloudless blue
With a banner-ad for seafood
Kite-tailing behind
Ripping like gunfire

As if Germany or Okinawa
He watches it circle once
And spitfire off
To strafe the beaches at Misquamicut

# Closing

The realtor calls
To shift the closing
On account of the buyers' interpreter

Who works at a seafood place on The Sound
*Open everyday but Thursday*
*Oh   and he's the owner*
*And the lone employee*

So that last Thursday in May   sun just up
We get on the highway
And arrive mid-morning
A couple blocks from City Hall

All of us with ballpoints
Around a brown table
While the attorney circulates
Documents for signatures
Explains in plain English
As the interpreter deciphers
And the buyers nod

Soon   abruptly almost

Chairs roll back
And that was that

I (being the oldest)
Go over to the new owners
Say I believe our parents are happy
Their home sold to folks
Who worked so hard   saved so long

I wish them the best
And when the translator finishes
They nod   smile slightly

In the parking lot
We   the late living evidence
Of our mother and father   talk
Tear up   as after a wake

And we carry that ache to our cars
And wave
And drive off separate ways

# 2

*. . . a momentary stay*
*against confusion.*

Robert Frost
*from* The Figure a Poem Makes

# Wordworking

1
It's good for a poem
To spend time in a drawer
Among crayons   3-in-One oil
Rose-scented soap

Keys on a ring   travel brochures
Scissors   receipts   menus
Glasses no longer strong enough

An old phone   old phonebook
Hex wrench   stray push pin
A blue band once wrapped around asparagus

Loose change   a green extension cord
Candles in case of emergency
Matches   knife sharpener   dust

Because you just never know

2
And because a poem
May be wounded

And two poems
Might talk all night
Like siblings in bunk beds

And poems are pictures
Painted with words

And free verse
Ain't really all that free

3
So you should probably wait
It can take a while

For words to work themselves
Into lines you might say out loud

Longer yet
For the perfect scar
Some poems are meant to form

## Note to a Young Poet

Sit with the scribbling of others   yes
And listen a lot

But make your own hay
Trim your own limbs
Drum your own drums
Hum your own hymns

And when sirens wail
Pull over   and pray
However you pray

May you always
'Sound like yourself'
And say less
Than there is to say

Let there be no end
To the blessings on your work

And once in a while   in life   in a poem
Take a ride
Just to see where you wind up

# Weather Eye

The sun slips out of town
    Past that sloped stand of oaks
        And sinks in time over the hills

A saint's darkness blooms
    Night runs its course
        Starless   without wind

And you feel
    Your morning will come up gray
        With mist and showers settling in

The way grief
    Gets together with regret
        And stays   and makes a day of it

# Brushwork

1
A weekday morning in April
Feeling like March still

And outside the diner
A man and woman embrace

A long embrace   traffic motoring by

The man says something
Reassures her maybe
Kisses her on the cheek

She goes to her car
He to his

2
Not something you see
This time of year
In a small Pennsylvania town

Bluestone skies
Wide swings in temperature
Most of us head down
And one foot in front of the other

Thank god
An artist witnessed them
From that little park
By the pork store

Somebody
Who paints daily wonders

Like the man's worn tan work coat
The woman's powder-blue puffer
Neither of them wearing gloves

Someone
Who knows the menu
And probably too the waitress

Standing by the door
In this unframed oil-on-board
Propped in the gallery window

Staring out
At the man and woman
In the parking lot

Holding each other

## Snow Day

Two girls at Ann Street Park
One in a light green jacket   with a shovel

The other in a red sweatshirt
That says *Lady Eagles*  with a ball

They clear part of the court
And talk and take shots

After a while
The sun breaks through
And the maples rain melting snow

And a few blocks over
A woman plans to leave
The one who swore to god
He wouldn't do it again

Now the girls make their way
Up Fifth Street
Turn left on Catharine
Talking the whole time

Middle-schoolers
Somebody's daughters

# Tupperware

Now's not the best time to die
'Cause there's a leak
Under the upstairs sink
You've told nobody about

Behind Q-tips   Drano   shampoo
You set out Tupperware
And empty it religiously

Imagine loved ones
Saying their final goodbyes
Hinting that maybe
You weren't so awful after all

Only to get home and find
Water pooling the entry hall
Bellying the ceiling above

Spurring them to wonder anew
About you   your 'priorities'
And   in particular   that list
You kept crossing out and adding to

Yeah   and wouldn't it be just like you
They'd conclude   to leave them
Sweating the next fiasco

Guessing what else you left unchecked's
Getting ready to blow

# Cheering

It's a Saturday game
Parents lean against the link fence
Stand in the bleachers

A young dad barks nonstop
And the umpire   a volunteer fireman   I think
Seems to sweat every call

I consider going over to the dad
When the inning ends to say
*I remember when an ump ruled*
*My son's first home run a double*
*And I yelled till he tossed me out*

Or kid him
About a support group
For parents of Little Leaguers
With catchy topics like

Deep Breathing Between Innings
The Yelling Cessation Workshop
Bogus Calls and Authority Issues
When the F-Word Slips Out
Losing and the Ice Cream After

But I can see he's wound too tightly
For laughs just now

The truth is
I see him   and see myself
Knowing so little as a dad
Trying like hell
To cover all the bases

My yelling wasn't
As hereditary as I'd once imagined
(Though the Irish *are* a mouthy bunch)

Give him time
He'll figure things out

So I say
*I can't believe my grown sons*
*Were once this small*
And leave it at that

# Last Roof

I meet with the roofer
On an Indian summer Friday
To upgrade our worn three-tabs
With something more 'architectural'

*The look of a roof is key*   he agrees
*Here's one style*
*Perfect for a house in town*

I'm drawn to the slate-like
Color   thickness   feel
And ask about warranty and price

He eyes me up and down   says
*You'll be in the ground*
*Long before you even think about*
*Replacing these shingles*
*Definitely your last roof*

*I want it nice*   I say
*But hey   it's not the Vatican*

*I got these*   he says (eyeing me sideways)
*Won't set you back so bad*
*But depending on how things go*
*You <u>could</u> be lookin' at replacement*
*Maybe   maybe not*

*Can I take both samples home*
*To talk things over with my wife*

*No problem*
*Have 'em for the weekend*  he says
*Gimme a shout on Mondee*
*Tuesdee's ok too*
*So we get ya done*
*Before snow flies*

*Yup   Lord Willing*
*Before snow flies*   I say   shutting the trunk
And   leaving well enough alone
Hold off asking
If he knows any good gutter guys

35

# Four Corners Upstate

*after Elizabeth Bishop*

1

Nothing for minutes
A truck may come
Or several cars

On the corner   in need of weeding
A planter   or rather
A tractor tire laid flat
And paint-brushed green

In the center
A single stout sunflower
Five feet high

So close to the road
It nods in the wake
Of a downshifting tractor trailer
And waves its tropical
Tobacco-sized leaves

Butterscotch mums spill
The tire's circumference

And   facing east   the sunflower
Draws many bees to its cheeks


2
What was it she meant
Who dreamt up
This very arrangement

Wasn't she the one
Who ran the store
And moved all of a sudden
Back to Baltimore


3
A dry September
And the head of the sunflower
Lowers and lowers

*Grand Opening*
Taped in the window still
A realtor's sign prongs the grass

Other signs call out
Nearby towns
And arrows point

*The Episcopal Church Welcomes*
*Orchard 3 Miles   Pick Your Own*

There's a sense you have
With the motor running
That given enough distance
Some things could be forgotten

If not forgotten
Forgiven maybe

# 3

*So let poems remember*
*What History dismisses*

# God's Acre

Remembrance Place Park
Milford, Pennsylvania

*Perhaps in this neglected spot is laid*
*Some heart once pregnant with celestial fire . . .*

from Elegy Written in a Country Churchyard
Thomas Gray   1751

1

So many unknowns
Above and below us

This park   a lost lot once
A graveyard for families
Going back lifetimes
With names we say today

For years   a neglected spot
Its mostly-marble headstones
Toppled   taken   flipped
Face down for walkways even

Or carted to the cemetery on the hill
Along with remains unearthed here
And reburied up there

Yet   remains remain still
Lord knows where

2

And lord knows
How they lived through those winters
When the river froze so thick
They could sled a house across it
From one state to the other

Lord knows
The hopes they clung to
Father   mother   worried sick
Over a newborn's cough and high fever
Mourning all the while their earlier loss

That arched stone in the grass
Half the average height and width
The word 'BABY' cut into it

3

Praise for this garden
And for its gardeners

And for what flowers   shrubs   and trees
Say about devotion

And for what these worn stones
Say about a small town

The way it goes on
Ending  and beginning again

And bless those
Who remember to remember

The sons and daughters
Of sons and daughters

Souls beyond names now
Locals to this day

## The Mitchells

1
A sign by the shale drive
Says 'Antiques'

Not a soul inside
The white clapboard church

Pews gone
Altar a thing of the past

And scrawled on card stock
Taped to a column

> *Last Days*
> *No Refunds*

2
Judging by what's left   a mishmash
Random stuff beyond repair

The last days look
Just about played-out

No hope for these picture frames
A dozen-or-so   dinged
Loose miters   cracked glass

A stained print of the Guggenheim
A curled watercolor of a tan cat
On a blue window sill

The rest empty   and pretty lame
Except for this one
Buried among the others
(Oddly   in good shape

And with that pale gold glow
Collectors find so desirable)
Holding an old family photo

3
Two sons   a daughter
The three of them grown
And standing behind
Their mother and father
Seated in front

You see the daughter in the mother
The sons in the father

All five are Quaker-faced
And dressed in Sunday best

As was the style in 1900
When   according to the note
On the back   this grayscale
Of the Mitchells was taken

Yet it wasn't till long after
(February 1970) when they were
Given a home in this frame
By a relative   distant and unnamed
Though the note's flowing strokes suggest
It was likely a woman

4
It's anyone's guess
How they went from keeping watch
In a descendant's stair hall

To leaning up against
This velveteen loveseat
Pocked with cigarette burns

In the company of uncollectibles
Set to be hauled away

End times for the lot of it
And you'd think by now

It might've crossed somebody's mind
To ditch the Mitchells
And make off with their frame
(For next-to-nothing   probably)

But   so far anyway
No one's had the heart

# To the Unremembered

1

I had a dream about Emily Dickinson
The only poet I've ever dreamt of
Except for that cameo by Robert Bly
In a nightmare   stemming no doubt
From the biscuits and chili I ate before bed

It felt as if she'd sent for me
And we never leave her room
Upstairs in her father's house
Overlooking the unpaved street

Afternoon   and it must be spring
Because she has her windows open
And the breeze is scented with lilac

She's in a long dark dress
(Not white   as some scholars assert)
And her voice is mild   familiar
(Not at all shrill   as other scholars claim)

More surprising
She laughs a lot   she's actually
Funnier than people think   kidding

About Austin and Susan   her brother and his wife
Who live   she points and says
*Right across the way*

Though   suddenly she stops
And watches without a word
As a woman who's lived a long time alone
Walks past with her two small dogs

2
The sun nearly down now
Amherst goes quiet
A carriage below   its horse clopping
Bells calling for vespers

Not the best time to ask
Why she writes
With so many dashes

And rather than taking up the question
Or maybe as a response to it
She places her hand on mine
Her left on my right   rests it there
The one time we touch
Then lights a candle

And all around   on the desk
Dresser   bed   in the corners even
Are paper bundles that weren't there earlier
Some tied with ribbons
Others with red yarn   or green string

Her shadows and reflections are everywhere
Somebody's on the stairs
And I wake up

3
Night after night
I'd read her poems
But found no way back

And came to imagine
Her hand on the hand
Of a different dreamer

Sister of the misfit
The heartsick
Those at a loss

She binds up wounds
And returns us to the world
To remember

The unremembered
The unmarked
The unremarkable

We who   like her
Keep our sabbaths at home
On scraps of paper

Unknown mostly
In our own lifetime
As she was unknown in hers

# Available Light   1913

1
On account of the darkness and the cold
The millwork shop closed earlier
And mice would have the run of the place
Until the first cabinetmaker returned before dawn

Every flat belt slipped
Every pulley threw frigid air
Until the stove could warm
The tools   the benches
The wood we carried in from the sheds

Joinery took longer
And money when we needed it most
Came slowest in winter


2
Like the rest of town
And the farms beyond town
I lived locally   went to bed early

And when it was my week
To light the stove
I walked to the shop

And snow would give off moonlight
And I was conscious of being alive
In time and timelessness
But I would keep such thoughts to myself


3
One December when it seemed
We might have no work
A minister (miraculously) gave us a deposit
To make white oak bookcases
A walnut desk and hall table

He'd come down from upstate
To comfort his sister
Who'd lost her child
And to pray with her husband
Who was caught torching the church

I remember wondering
How many books he must've read
To keep his hope so well-honed
And thinking he'd probably say
*Just the one Book*

Because he was young
And sure of purpose
Which must have been a godsend
For the members of his flock
Gathered as they were
At one end of a frozen Finger Lake

# Breaktime on the Jersey Jobsite

1
A serious project
For some money-guy
From the City

Back a good distance
Barely visible now
Even with the leaves down

Inside   a salamander spews
Fuel-smelling heat
Through the open stud walls

And the tin-knocker's
Boom box fumes
Somewhere in the basement

Snow starts again
Flurrying past the rough openings
Tacked with plastic

As we gather
In the space the blueprints say
Is the Great Room

Stone fireplace   cathedral ceiling
Panels   beams   collar-ties
Feeling more like a lodge than a chapel

Our table   a bowed   banged-up
Piece of fir plywood on sawhorses
With a fair bit of sway

Set around with brown
Fold-up chairs
Lugged from job to job


2
Like yesterday
And the day before
Our talk takes off

The mason swerving on his way here
To avoid a buck
In the middle of 202
*Big as a friggin' moose*

Some Center in the NBA
Making obscene money
And missing more and more free-throws

The framer's father   88 last week
And living by himself   forgets
His steak on the stove
Fire department comes   and him yelling
*Only way I'm movin's*
*When they carry me out in a box*

Crooked politicians
Trading stocks before the vote
That pumps or tanks them

The plumber's ex *shacked up*
*With some jackass from Hackensack*
And the kids are a mess
A boy   17   looking to quit school
A girl   only 14
And already threatening a tattoo

Architects who have *absolutely no clue*

The electrician says
*Donny the laborer*
*Who fell from a scaffold*
*On that job in Woodcliff Lake's*
*Gonna be alright   but'll*

*Probly limp the rest of his life*
*Coulda' been one-hell-of-a-lot worse*
*Helps to be young*

Caffeine speeds the speech
And the poetry goes and goes
One man   then another
Saying what he's seen
Telling what he knows

# Here and Hereafter

*. . . the past years*
*Assume their solemn place one by one*

*from* Elegy For The Monastery Barn
Thomas Merton   1953

1
Consider the lilies   for sure

Consider too
The lightning rods
At either end of the roof

That eagle
Atop the cupola
Copper-gone-green   wings spread

The barn below
Hay piled high inside
Generations coming and going

An empty temple now
Sway-backed   missing windows
Its south side sliding doors
Racked off-track

2
Consider the crew
From two states away

And how   by the end
Of a really long week in May

They've loaded posts   beams
Boards   doors   jambs   pegs
Hooks   harnesses   horseshoes
Buckets of cut nails
Hinges caked with rust

*Reclaimed*   they say
*Better than feeding flames*
And all the rage these days
For upscale family rooms   kitchens
A hotel bar in the city even

The eagle bubble-wrapped
Boxed up for auction

And   hand-and-horse-dug
The old foundation's filled in
Graded   raked   seeded
Tossed with loose hay

The tall catalpas
The rutted path
The cow pond downhill
All left looking out of place

## Land of the Living

Before the town wakes
Before thinking gets going

Out of the corner of my eye
A chipmunk stretches up the mesh fence
Up the round post   over and in
Through the hole in the house
Where bluebirds lived till late last week

A cardinal sails through the yard
Tucks into a shrub above the wall
Then flutters out   all red
Across the banks of lupine
Foxglove   coreopsis   oxeye daisies
Off into the woods

The usual groundhog   the usual rabbit
That mostly-black cat
And already a handful
Of the neighbor's honey bees
Sipping at our fountain's dripping top lip

This   as the moon fades
And the sun becomes more sure of itself
Orioles call and answer   call and answer

Trees swell uphill

The whole place coming to life
And me   for the moment   just here
All eyes and ears

Apart from my name
    and taking no measure
    and making no claim

# Coda

*As he came forth*
*Of his mother's womb*
*Naked shall he return*
*To go as he came*

*And shall take*
*Nothing of his labour*
*Which he may carry away*
*In his hand*

Ecclesiastes
5:15, KJV

## Sister Cities

Days of thundering surf
And the sea's finally at ease

A full moon lays light
Along the tide   the beach   dune grass
And glows the trunks
And tips of the palms

Across the water
An ignorant army
With a history of domestic violence
Pounds the hospitals and schools
Sister cities
Flesh of its own flesh

The sea *is* calm tonight
Country music drifts
Down from the balcony above
And someone's cooking with curry
No emergency vehicles wailing by
And stocks seem headed
For all-time highs

But the shelling we see
Hits too close to home
Might as well be
Pummeling loved ones up the coast

# Always the Women

Men gather

And some of them
Come away thinking things

Saying what's what
Telling everybody how it is

    what righteousness looks like
    what transgression looks like

    big god   little god
    one persuasion or another

    setting up sovereignties   borderlands
    red flags   lines in sand

    by hook or crook
    by bell   book   or candle

    and so on
    and so forth

history in a nutshell

And always the women
Running with their babies

# The Hallowed Man

1

Twelve days after Christmas

For centuries

Three Kings Day

Feast of the Epiphany

And now

An unholy day

Another in our history

'Which will live in infamy'

Feast of the 'Rough Beast'

Cult-confederacy of conspiracy

armed to the teeth with untruth

With a gospel

of grievance and disunion

Spun by the hallowed man

the chosen one

High-rise messiah
    preaching to the choir


2

*I alone can fix it* he barks

        *'Mine eyes have seen the glory'*
            (they reply)

*Make for Bethlehem on the run* he yowls
*Hurry for the Second Coming*

        *'He hath loosed the fateful lightning'*
            (they proclaim)

Shoving up the temple steps
Bashing their way in

        *'Trampling out the vintage*
     *Where the grapes of wrath are stored'*
            (they believe)

Hearts hollowed out
Heads stuffed
    with a fraud-god's

           'dark light'


3

In the name of the father
In the name of the son
In the name of the neighbor
    the uncle   the brother   the friend
        living in anger
           we pray

In the name of the ancestors
In the name of the woman and the child
In the name of those to come
           we pray

In the name of all that's holy
Deliver them from wolves
    in men's clothing

Help them find
    better gods

We ask this
Knowing how wolves
    circle and lie in wait

We ask
Knowing a wolf's no wolf
    without followers

*This is the way the world mends*
*This is the way the world mends*
*This is the way the world mends*
*Not with a bang   but together*

# Notes

### Whereabouts  Pg.2

The first public reading of this poem was at the Milford Theater on July 16, 2022, for 'The Water Gap; Return to the Homeland,' introduced by Daniel StrongWalker Thomas, Hereditary Chief of the Lenape Tribe, sponsored by Grey Towers Heritage Association.

It's not clear (by design) who the poem's speaker is. Or was. We might imagine these words were discovered in the journal of a descendant of one of the early settlers, for example. Though it could also be the voice of a present-day Lenape elder — telling what happened.

### Miserere  Pg.8

Miserere: Latin. 'Be Merciful.'

### Note to a Young Poet  Pg.22

The title's a reference to Rilke's 'Letters to a Young Poet.'

'Sound Like Yourself': from Kurt Vonnegut's 'How to Write with Style.'

### God's Acre  Pg.36

God's Acre: an early term for a cemetery.

Remembrance Place Park (sometimes called The Old Dimmick Cemetery) is located in Milford Borough at the corner of West Ann Street and Elderberry Alley.

### Sister Cities  Pg.60

'An ignorant army.' 'The sea *is* calm tonight.' Both phrases echo Matthew Arnold's poem 'Dover Beach.'

## The Hallowed Man  Pg.68

The poem's title is a reference to T.S. Eliot's 'The Hollow Men', published in 1925, and the epigraph is taken from the final stanza of section 1.

'An unholy day' . . . January 6, 2021, when the United States Capitol Building in Washington, D.C. was attacked by a mob — thousands of rioters who believed the false claim that the 2020 presidential election was 'stolen.'

'Which will live in infamy' from an address given on December 8, 1941, by President Franklin D. Roosevelt to a joint session of congress one day after the United States was attacked by Japan.

'Rough Beast', Bethlehem and the Second Coming allude to W.B Yeats's 'The Second Coming', published in 1920.

'Mine eyes have seen the glory'

'He hath loosed the fateful lightning'

'Trampling out the vintage
Where the grapes of wrath are stored'

> *from* The Battle Hymn of the Republic
> Julia Ward Howe  1862

'Dark Light' from 'Treatise On Theology' (Section10, We Have Read In the Catechism), a poem by Czeslaw Milosz (trans. Robert Hass): 'Lucifer, bearer of dark light' . . .

'This is the way the world mends' . . . a variation on the 'nursery rhyme' last stanza of Eliot's poem, which reads: 'This is the way the world ends'.

# Acknowledgments

I'm grateful

To Celeste: First Listener.

To Eamon Grennan for reading my work over these years.
And for his own extraordinary collections, which teach on
the page how (as in 'The Cave Painters') we 'come to terms
with the given world', and how, like them, we might 'leave
something upright and bright behind' us.

To Sean Strub, Mayor of Milford, who proposed the
position of Poet Laureate to the Milford Borough Council.
And to members of the Council who appointed me.
Seamus Heaney was exactly right when he said: 'The aim of
poetry and the poet is finally to be of service, to ply the effort
of the individual into the larger work of the community as
a whole.'

To Daniel StrongWalker Thomas, Hereditary Chief of the
Lenape Tribe, who introduced the first public reading of
'Whereabouts' at the Milford Theater.

To local Pike County Publications: The Journal, The
Courier, The Dispatch.

To Milford: its citizens, wide streets, alleys, parks,
architecture, hills, creeks, river . . .

    'The way it goes on
    Ending  and beginning  again'

74

## Remembering

Charles and Cecelia O'Neil

Tommy O'Neil

Stephen Fuqua, III

Tim Fuqua

Mary Ann Fuqua

Stephen O. and Frances Fuqua

# About The Author

Chuck O'Neil has written five poetry collections, most recently *better gods*. He lives in Milford, Pennsylvania, where he and his wife, Celeste, have lived since 1982. They have four children and three grandchildren. In 2022 he was named Poet Laureate of Milford.

Photo by Marie Liu

www.chuckoneilauthor.com